Napoleon's Guns 1792–1815 (2)

Heavy and Siege Artillery

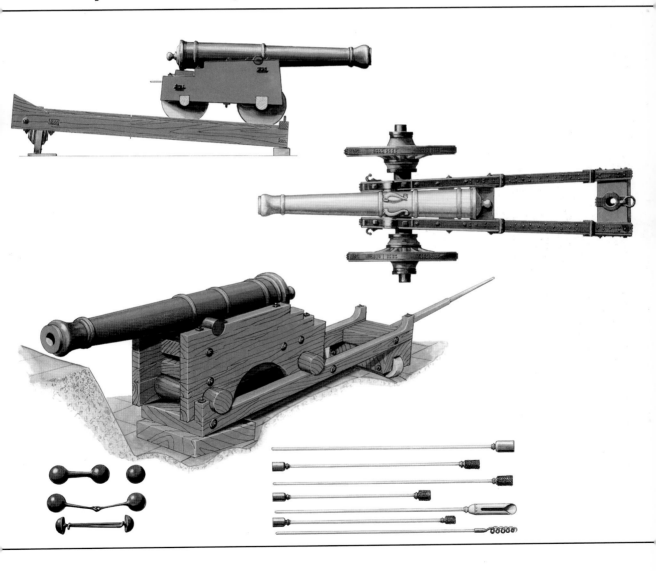

René Chartrand · Illustrated by Ray Hutchins

First published in Great Britain in 2003 by Osprey Publishing, Elms Court, Chapel Way, Botley, Oxford OX2 9LP, United Kingdom.
Email: info@ospreypublishing.com

ISBN 1 84176 460 4

Editorial: Ilios Publishing, Oxford, UK (www.iliospublishing.com)
Design: Melissa Orrom Swan
Index by Alison Worthington
Originated by Electronic Page Company, Cwmbran, UK
Printed in China through World Print Ltd.

A CIP catalogue record for this book is available from the British Library.

03 04 05 06 07   10 9 8 7 6 5 4 3 2 1

For a catalogue of all books published by Osprey Military and Aviation please contact:

Osprey Direct UK, P.O. Box 140, Wellingborough, Northants, NN8 2FA, UK
E-mail: info@ospreydirect.co.uk

Osprey Direct USA, c/o MBI Publishing, P.O. Box 1, 729 Prospect Ave, Osceola, WI 54020, USA
E-mail: info@ospreydirectusa.com

www.ospreypublishing.com

Artist's note

Readers may care to note that the original paintings from which the colour plates in this book were prepared are available for private sale. The Publishers retain all reproduction copyright whatsoever. All enquiries should be addressed to:

Ray Hutchins, 57/59 Huntley Lane, Huntley, Cheadle, Staffordshire ST10 1UA

The Publishers regret that they can enter into no correspondence upon this matter.

Measures and Weights

The French official measures used from 1668 to 1840 were:
2 miles to 1 lieue = 3.898km
1000 toises to 1 mile = 1.949km
6 feet to 1 toise = 1.949m
12 inches to 1 foot = 32.484cm
12 lines to 1 inch = 2.707cm
12 points to 1 line = 2.256mm
1 point = 0.188mm
It is important for British and American readers to note that the French distances of 'miles' and 'feet' were not the same as the Imperial measures used in Britain and her colonies, as well as in the United States. The French mile was equal to 1.949km compared to 1.61km for the English; the French foot equals 32.484cm compared to 30.48cm for the English foot.
The calibre of French Artillery was measured by the diameter of the ball, as opposed to the British who measured it by the diameter of the bore.
The system of French weights used from 1350 to 1840 was somewhat heavier than the British Avoirdupois system used from 1582:
1 livre (pound) = 16 onces (ounces) = 489.41g (453.6g to 1 British pound)
1 once (ounce) = 576 grains = 30.588g (28.35g to 1 British ounce)

NAPOLEON'S GUNS 1792–1815 (2) HEAVY AND SIEGE ARTILLERY

INTRODUCTION

The phrase 'Napoleon's Guns' brings to mind the French field artillery present at all the famous battles fought by the French armies from the early 1790s to 1815. This arm of service can be seen in hundreds of battle paintings, and its exploits are recorded in numerous publications. And yet, besides the justly famous field guns, the artillery also comprised the heavy guns used during sieges, in garrisons, and for coastal defence. These have attracted much less attention.

In order to be truly effective, heavy artillery had to be very accurately served. From the time that the first massive pieces of ordnance were cast in the later Middle Ages, the challenge was not only to shoot them, but also to transport them and mount them securely in fortifications, all of which required vast amounts of animal and manpower. For centuries, gunners struggled with the variable quality of black powder as a propellant for projectiles, calculated the best angles and diameters for range and hitting power, and made improvements to the guns themselves. At their best, siege artillery pieces could pound the stone wall of a fortress to rubble and make a breach, or shatter an enemy's siege batteries. However, it was not easy to handle and aim these big guns, especially within the confines of a fortress, until Jean Baptiste de Gribeauval devised some novel solutions for these problems.

There was an impressive variety, and source of origin, of the ordnance used by the heavy artillery of the French Army during the Revolutionary and Napoleonic Wars. The more secure inland fortifications might mount the heavy Vallière brass ordnance, with its elaborate mouldings reflecting the glory of Louis XV, gorgeous examples of 18th-century art, but outclassed because of their weight by the new artillery designed by Gribeauval from the 1760s onwards. Even heavier iron naval guns were used for coastal fortresses and batteries in both France and the colonies.

Austrian siege guns. Note the difference between the ornate gun cast in 1682 (top) and the clean-lined 24-pdr of 1756 (bottom) following the principles of Austria's director-general of artillery, Prince Liechtenstein. Gribeauval encountered this type of artillery design when he served with the Austrians and it greatly influenced the system he later created. (Print after R. von Ottenfeld)

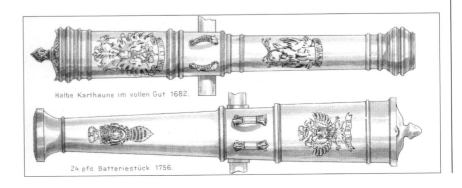

Halbe Karthaune im vollen Gut 1682.

24. pfd. Batteriestück 1756.

THE ARTILLERY COMMITTEE

In the first volume of this series (New Vanguard 66: *Napoleon's Guns 1792–1815 (1) Field Artillery*, Osprey, Oxford, 2003) the political context leading to the adoption of both the Gribeauval and the Year XI systems was outlined. It is also important to have an understanding of the activities of the important Comité de l'Artillerie set up by Napoleon. In 1776, King Louis XVI created the post of First Inspector-General of the Artillery and named General Gribeauval as the first incumbent, a post he held until his death in 1789. Gribeauval's passing away, combined with the outbreak of the French Revolution, led to the abandonment of the post. The French National Assembly announced the formation of an Artillery Committee in 1790, but it did not meet until five years later. The committee was supposed to ensure the technical quality of castings, as well as coordinate construction procedures through a number of senior inspecting artillery officers. In practice, as these officers were always serving with the army in the field, nothing much was done. Furthermore, the committee as set up by the National Assembly only had a consulting role, without any real power or authority. As a result the artillery had no real direction to ensure its technical excellence. This changed following Napoleon's arrival as First Consul. To give the committee more executive power, Napoleon revived the post of First Inspector-General and appointed General François-Marie d'Aboville to the job in 1800. A veteran of the battle of Fontenoy (1745) and the siege of Yorktown (1781), d'Aboville was a fine choice, if somewhat too elderly at the age of 70 to have the necessary vigour for the job. In 1802, Napoleon gave a senate seat to d'Aboville and named the youthful General (later Marshal) Auguste Marmont as the new First Inspector-General.

Although critics hinted that Marmont did not have much experience with artillery, he certainly brought energy to the post. Not content with inspecting the existing system, he felt that a new one should be designed to improve and replace the Gribeauval system. The result of this was that a whole new system of guns was designed by Colonel François de Fautrier to replace the Gribeauval system in 1803, Year XI of the French Revolutionary calendar. The other members of the committee did not unanimously approve of the new design, with the influential generals Jean-Jacques Gassendi and Nicolas-Marie de Songis leading the opposition. The Year XI heavy and garrison artillery designs were particularly disastrous and hardly any were made. The few heavy guns of the Year XI model that were cast ended up as curiosities in museums. One of the reasons for the failure of the Year XI system was the lack of communication by Marmont. He obviously assumed that his seniority

François-Marie, Comte d'Aboville (1730–1817), was only 14 when he entered the artillery. By the time of the American Revolution he had become an experienced lieutenant-colonel and was selected to lead the artillery with Rochambeau's army in America. His efficient use of the new Gribeauval system at Yorktown was a major cause of its surrender, for which he was promoted to brigadier-general. In 1792, he again played an important part in the French victory at Valmy that brought him the rank of lieutenant-general. Napoleon had a high regard for d'Aboville and gave him the post of First Inspector-General of the Artillery in 1800. This was perhaps too much for the elderly gunner and, in 1802, he was appointed a senator.

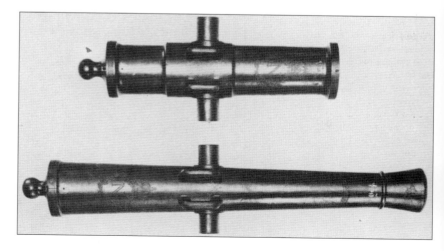

Gribeauval siege 24-pdr from the 1770s. Right side view. The carriage's long trail is particularly distinctive. This replica is located at Yorktown, Virginia. (Photo RC)

LEFT **Year XI 5 inch 6 lines (or 24-pdr) brass field howitzer (above) and a Year XI brass 6-pdr field cannon (below) in the Royal Danish Arsenal Museum, both engraved with Napoleon's crowned 'N' and surrounded by a wreath. As a whole, these were the only pieces of the Year XI (1803) system to have gone further than the drawing board and were cast in some quantity for issue to the army, mostly between 1804 and 1809.**

would ensure its success regardless. However, in a subject as sensitive and highly technical as artillery, the potential for battlefield failure as well as the enormous costs involved ensured that a number of different points of view needed to be considered. In any event, Marmont was promoted to a field command in 1804, while important data failed to be shared. As late as February 1806, General Gassendi reported to the Minister of War that the construction tables had not been communicated by the First Inspector-General to the ministry's artillery division, and that tests had been conducted improperly; some had not been done and for those that were, the officers finding faults had been put under pressure to remain silent. So, in practice, the Gribeauval system heavy guns remained those in use. In 1804, General de Songis became the First Inspector-General. General Jean-Ambroise Lariboisière replaced him in 1810 and, by early 1814, Napoleon had to take over the committee's leadership.[1] He passed on the actual work to the Minister of War Marshal Henri Clarke, who reorganised the committee into three sections. But this was the last year of Napoleon's reign, and little further could be done to improve artillery technology.

During the last decade of Napoleon's reign, the committee's work was more concerned with routine matters than technical innovation. The senior bureaucrats in the Ministry of War manoeuvred priorities so as to keep executive decisions in their own hands, leaving the committee members only an advisory role. This was relatively easy to do as many were serving in the field, far from Paris. Thus, while French artillery officers recommended a series of improvements to the system, based upon experiences in the field, nothing was done. For instance, in March 1810, Brigadier General François Berge praised the brass used to cast guns in Sevilla, as it produced weapons that could fire over 5,000 shots before being worn out. This feat was attributed to Peruvian copper, but even this did not shake the Ministry of War's preference for Russian copper, which was considered purer. Strangely, some experiments with English copper were ordered at this time. Also from Spain was the observation that the British were using iron 24-pdr heavy siege guns rather than brass ones. These guns could shoot up to 20 shots an hour (rather than five) to a distance of 600m, rather than 400m. They were also considerably lighter than the French ordnance. Still another British innovation was the lethal projectile invented by General Shrapnel, first used at Vimeiro, Portugal, in August 1808. The French held some

1 General Lariboisière died on 25 December 1813. and was replaced by General Jean-Baptiste Eblé by an order of Napoleon, dated in Paris on 3 January 1814. However, General Eblé had died on 30 December 1813 at Königsberg (Prussia), so that Napoleon took on the leadership of the committee. On the committee's history, see: Pierre Nardin, 'Le comité de l'artillerie et ses réalisations des origines à 1870', *Revue Internationale d'Histoire Militaire*, No. 82, 2002.

inconclusive experiments with this sort of shell in 1812, but nothing came of it and the Shrapnel shell was not adopted until the late 1830s. Thus, Napoleon's aim of giving more executive power to the Artillery Committee in 1800 fell by the wayside. One reason was that occupants of the post of First Inspector-General did not have the inventive genius of Gribeauval. Another reason was that, except for Marmont, the later First Inspector-Generals did not have the seniority to impose their will. Finally, it must be noted that Napoleon, who was much preoccupied by other questions, left the committee in something of a limbo. The end result was that Gribeauval's system remained in use throughout the Napoleonic period with no major innovations brought in as far as heavy artillery was concerned.

TYPES OF ORDNANCE

The Gribeauval system siege and garrison artillery consisted of 24-, 16-, 12- and 8-pdr guns; 8-inch siege howitzers; 12-, 10- and 8-inch siege and garrison mortars (with cylindrical chambers); 12-, 10- and 8-inch siege and garrison Gomer mortars (with truncated conical chambers); and a 15-inch stone mortar.

Unlike the field pieces, the heavy artillery in Gribeauval's system incorporated some of the older designs. The 8-inch siege howitzer was Vallière's basic design adapted by Gribeauval for siege operations. The 8-, 12- and 15-inch mortars were also appropriated into the new Gribeauval system. The 12-inch mortar was also from the old Vallière system; existing pieces were taken into Gribeauval's system, though any newly built 12-inch mortars were to be reinforced by another 300 pounds of brass.

Guns

Gribeauval's system of heavy artillery was less obviously superior to the system it replaced when compared to his improvements to the field artillery. The first test performed in 1764 did not seem to show a marked superiority for Gribeauval's higher calibre guns compared to existing older weaponry. The problem with Vallière's heavy guns, as with his field pieces, was their great weight. Gribeauval's guns were much lighter, and so they were officially adopted in 1765.

Although Gribeauval system guns were cast during the 1760s, there was still some controversy surrounding their effectiveness, especially regarding the heavier 'garrison' 8-, 12-, 16- and 24-pdrs. As these were intended to arm fortresses as garrison pieces, and their weight did not matter very much as they were mounted in fixed position, Gribeauval's critics maintained that there was little point in going to the expense of casting them. The debate went on and, in 1786, further tests of the Gribeauval designs for 16- and 24-pdr garrison guns were made. These tests proved to be inconclusive. The tolerance of the

Another view of a Gribeauval siege 24-pdr from the 1770s. This replica is also based at Yorktown, Virginia. (Photo RC)

24-pdr, as cast by the foundry of the reputable Potevin brothers, was especially disappointing, with some barrels only lasting 100 shots before suffering some stress damages. Under these circumstances, and bearing in mind the high cost of casting such heavy pieces in brass, production ceased until the French Revolution.

The main features of the Gribeauval heavy artillery guns were:

CALIBRE	LENGTH	WEIGHT
8-pdr gun (106.1mm)	285cm	1,060kg
12-pdr gun (121.3mm)	317cm	1,550kg
16-pdr gun (133.7mm)	336cm	2,000kg
24-pdr gun (152.7mm)	353cm	2,740kg
Long 4-pdr gun* (84.0mm)	235cm	560kg

(* This type of gun was not officially part of the Gribeauval system, but some were cast at Douai in 1792. Its use appears to have been very limited.)

The 8- and 12-pdr guns were longer and heavier than the field pieces of the same calibre. A heavy 8-pdr measured 285cm and weighed 1,060kg, compared to a field 8-pdr that was 200cm long and weighed 580kg. A heavy 12-pdr was 317cm long with a weight of 1,550kg, whereas the field 12-pdr had a length of 229cm and a weight of 880kg. The dimensions were essentially the same as the guns of the 1732 Vallière system, except that there were fewer mouldings and other decorative elements.

The 4-pdrs might be the type cast at Douai in the 1790s, but were more likely to be simply field 4-pdrs mounted on travelling carriages. Such guns were especially handy in a besieged fortress, as they could be moved easily and rapidly from one place to the other.

By the time the French Revolutionary War broke out in 1792, the distinction between siege and garrison artillery had become largely academic. By then, the accepted wisdom regarding firepower and range was in favour of heavy calibres: the heavier the calibre, the longer the range. Thus, not only would a larger calibre deliver a heavier round but also, because of the distance, it might be done with increased safety from enemy fire. The long 8- and 12-pdrs were now used as armament within fortresses.

The range of 16- and 24-pdr guns made them especially useful to the garrisons of besieged fortresses. A 16-pdr at a 45-degree elevation could fire at targets up to 4,300m away, a 24-pdr at the same elevation could reach 4,800m. These ranges could also be increased if the besieged town occupied

Gribeauval siege 24-pdr from the 1770s. Viewed from the rear. Note that squared 'handles' were also seen on top of the Gribeauval system heavy guns, just as on the field artillery pieces, although the original design plates showed the more Baroque-looking 'dolphins' on top of the brass guns. This replica is located at Yorktown, Virginia. (Photo RC)

a commanding height over the surrounding countryside. This long-range capacity could create many problems for a besieging enemy if they placed their magazines and artillery park too close. The 12- and 8-pdrs had a range of about 4,000m and 3,500m respectively, and could not compete with the heavier guns, especially if they were located in siege batteries beneath the town. Only if the besieging army had some 16- and 24-pdrs (or some heavy guns of approximate calibre) in its batteries would the odds be more even. Indeed, it was almost essential to have such pieces for a siege to be successful, but they were slow and cumbersome to move around.

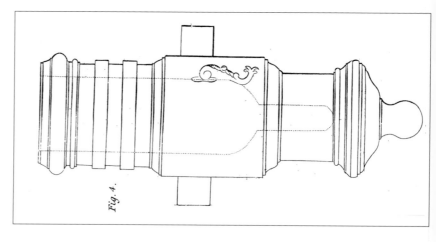

The siege artillery also included the old 8-inch (223mm) howitzers, weighing 540kg with a length of 94cm. They were designed by General Vallière and first cast in 1749. The 8-inch howitzers were too heavy for much use in the field, and they were relegated to siege and garrison use by Gribeauval. They were effective to a range of 3,200m at a 45-degree elevation, but howitzers were mainly intended for ricochet fire. At a six-degree angle, a howitzer shell would first hit the ground at about 830m, at ten degrees about 1,200m.

The next step in the development of the French artillery was the introduction of the 'Year XI' system in 1803. The only additions to the heavy artillery were a long 12-pdr gun and a short 24-pdr gun. These heavy guns were not a priority and very few were cast. On the whole, Napoleon's heavy artillery inland remained of the Gribeauval system.

There were some exceptions to this rule, a notable example being the very heavy ordnance used by the French against Cadiz in 1811. This great port had come under siege in 1810, and was valiantly defended by a Spanish garrison with British and Portuguese reinforcements. Hoping to break the resistance of the city by a long-range heavy bombardment, the French decided to make two large pieces of artillery for the purpose. On another occasion, the French cast large 9-, 10- and 11-inch 'gun-howitzers' in brass at Sevilla. They were very heavy, weighing from 3,500kg to about 9,000kg, and were mounted on 250kg to 500kg carriages. They had a range of 6,000m, but were of limited use due to the difficulty of moving them because of their enormous bulk. A further attempt was made to cast a large piece of ordnance at Liège in 1813, this time out of iron, but nothing much resulted from this experiment.

Mortars

These weapons, which were used to shoot exploding bombs, were the subject of a great deal of experimentation in the 17th century, but then remained relatively the same during most of the 18th century. They were rightly considered to be the most dangerous type of ordnance to serve, as well as being the most complicated. Even with the best

The 8-inch howitzer was an integral part of the arsenal of Napoleonic siege and garrison artillery. Howitzers of this calibre were originally designed by Vallière in 1748 and retained when the Gribeauval system was adopted in the 1760s. They were used to shoot exploding shells and anti-personnel case shot, as well as ordinary round shot. The shells were fixed to a wooden shoe and put in the barrel by hand. The case shot consisted of five layers of 14 balls each and would ideally be fired at 'point blank' (*but-en-blanc*) range, c. 250m. (Print after Tousard)

A Gomer mortar, dating from the 1790s, with a gunner standing guard. (Print after Raffet)

precautions, the mortars were prone to fire prematurely and the bombs explode accidentally. This was because a mortar was really fired twice: first, the bomb had to be shot and propelled to descend over its target and, secondly, the bomb had a fuse that had to be lit so that it would explode just over the heads of the enemy.

To succeed, a specialised class of experienced and fearless artillerymen was required: the bombardiers. They were the highest paid and most respected group of artillerymen. Their duty was to ensure that the correct charges sent the bomb over the target, and that the fuse they had prepared would be lit and ignite its charge causing the bomb to explode at just the right moment. When it worked correctly the mortar bombs could cause many injuries or else set fire to buildings if they burst over the rooftops.

Until the middle of the 18th century, the bombardiers would have to ignite the fuse on the top of the bomb separately to the powder charge in the mortar. Needless to say, this procedure was both dangerous and difficult. At some point it was noticed that the powder ignited in the chamber could set fire to the fuse if the bomb in the chamber was given some narrow windage. This allowed the fire to spread around the lower half of the bomb and ignite the fuse. This allowance of a slight amount of windage all around was done by simply resting the bomb on small wooden stocks in the chamber that allowed the ignited gases to bypass. This process occurred within a fraction of a second and the bomb was propelled with its fuse ignited.

General Vallière had brought in a standard design for army mortars in 1732 when he introduced 8-inch and 12-inch pieces. They were used for the next several decades. By the 1750s, they were heavily criticised for their weight and lacklustre performance. They were subjected to a series of rigorous trials against the mortars of the Gribeauval system in 1765 and 1766. Gribeauval's design for mortars was very clean and devoid of almost any ornaments in marked contrast to Vallière's design. The tests put an end to the pear-shaped chamber design, as the recoil was so great as to severely damage the mortar's bed, thus rendering the piece almost useless. Henceforth, the army adopted mortars with cylindrical chambers. (The navy, however, retained pear-shaped mortars as described below.)

The durability of mortars was also tested at the time and it was found that 12-inch mortars in particular were incapable of resisting many more than 200 long-range (c. 2,400m) firings before they became unserviceable. They were liable to crack, which could cause the bomb to explode prematurely at great risk to the bombardiers. The new

Gribeauval 12-inch mortars were therefore made some 150kg heavier in order to be stronger. As a longer-term solution to this problem, Gribeauval opted to reduce the calibre of these mortars to 10 inches and to strengthen the bombs. The tests on this new mortar proved Gribeauval right, as their range exceeded 2,400m and their durability was greatly increased.

The mortars of the Gribeauval system were:

TYPE	LENGTH	WEIGHT
8-inch mortar (223.3mm)	58cm	270kg
10-inch short mortar (274.0mm)	74cm	780kg
10-inch long mortar (274.0mm)	81cm	980kg
12-inch mortar (324.8mm)	81cm	1,540kg

Although an improvement on the previous system, the new Gribeauval mortars were still far from perfect. The cylindrical chamber was not ideal as the mortar bomb tended to rest to one side when the tube was at the usual 45-degree inclination. This left a slight space for uneven windage to escape when the mortar was fired. The gases released by the explosion therefore put undue stress on the lower part of the chamber, and forced the bomb along one side of the chamber as it came out. When fired many times, this process caused the chamber to deteriorate and the mortar became rapidly unusable, even if reinforced. Accuracy was also affected as the uneven distribution of the exploding gases made the precise projection of the bomb towards its target slightly random. It should be noted that all chamber designs of the period suffered from this type of flaw. Gribeauval's cylindrical design was better than most, though it did not totally solve the problem.

Experiments with different types of mortar chambers continued for 20 years until 1785 when General de Gomer introduced a chamber shaped like a truncated cone. Gomer's chamber ensured that the bomb fitted snugly, thus eliminating windage. This increased the propellent power of the explosion, eliminated the undue pressure on a part of the chamber, and increased accuracy due to the equal distribution of the gases projecting the bomb. The Gomer mortars with

Siege mortar being loaded. Note how the piece points upright at the early stages of the procedure. The uniforms of the gunners date from 1775 but the manoeuvre was similar during the Napoleonic Wars. (Print after Moltzheim. Anne S.K. Brown Military Collection, Brown University, USA. Photo RC)

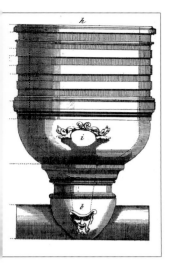

The brass 15-inch stone mortar was introduced in 1732 and incorporated into the Gribeauval system in 1765. This mortar had a very wide bore as it was designed as an anti-personnel weapon to project showers of stones on the attackers of a fortress. (Print after Le Blond)

their conical chamber design were adopted into the Gribeauval system in 1789. They were:

TYPE	LENGTH	WEIGHT
8-inch Gomer mortar (223.3mm)	55cm	290kg
10-inch Gomer mortar (274mm)	78cm	930kg
12-inch Gomer mortar (224.8mm)	90cm	1,300kg

One further mortar that formed part of the system was the ancient 15-inch (406.1mm) stone mortar, weighing 735kg. This was an anti-personnel weapon, usually set up in a fort, that fired showers of stones at close range, *c*. 180–200m. Its weight was inferior to that of other large mortars, as its chamber did not have to stand the same stress from propellent gases as a bomb-firing mortar.

As there was a shortage of mortars during the wars of the Revolution, an even more novel way to shoot 10-inch bombs was found by using a 16-pdr gun. Its breech was rested against a beam embedded in the ground, the bomb tied to the muzzle with thin strings and the gun pointed to an angle of 40 to 45 degrees. It may not have been extremely accurate but it basically did the job.

By the time Napoleon became emperor of the French in 1804, mortars were plentiful. Foundries were constantly casting them in numbers and there were also many that came from the captured artillery parks of vanquished enemies. Some of these countries had adopted the Gribeauval system so that calibres and weights were approximately the same. One innovation was the addition of some 6-inch and 8-inch mortars, a result of the foreign influence, notably from Austria and Prussia, on the French artillery from about 1808. These were usually foreign pieces pressed into French service and were not integral parts of the Gribeauval or the Year XI systems.

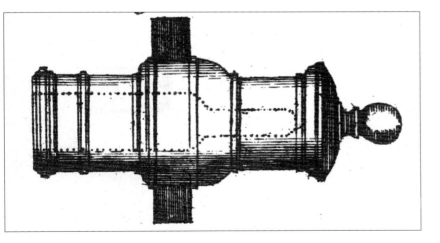

An 8-inch brass howitzer design of the mid-18th century. (Print after Le Blond)

CARRIAGES

The carriages for the French army's Gribeauval system siege guns were superficially quite similar to the carriages for the field guns. They were simply enlarged to accommodate the longer and heavier pieces of ordnance they had to support. The naves of the wheels had brass boxes within and the axletrees' spindles were covered with iron plates. For heavy guns, wooden quoins (wedges) were used as opposed to elevating screws and there were no 'travelling' trunnion sockets. Because of the great weight, siege guns were often carried separately from their carriages, the two being assembled once the town to be besieged was reached. There were no ammunition boxes between the cheeks as with the lighter field pieces as such items would have been too heavy and cumbersome.

The basic dimensions of the siege carriages were:

16-PDR SIEGE CARRIAGE

Length of the cheeks: 11ft 6in. (373.9cm).
Width of the cheeks: 5ft (162.4cm).
Height of the cheeks (at the aim curve): 1ft 2in. (379mm).
Height of the wheels: 4ft 10in. (157cm).

24-PDR SIEGE CARRIAGE

Length of the cheeks: 12ft (389.8cm).
Width of the cheeks: 5ft 6in. (178.6mm).
Height of the cheeks (at the aim curve): 1ft 3in. (406mm).
Height of the wheels: 4ft 10in. (157cm).

Curiously, the tables of construction given by De Scheel and Gassendi do not include a carriage for the 8-inch howitzer. Judging from its weight of 540kg, the carriage was probably fairly similar to that for the 8-pdr field gun that weighed 580kg (see New Vanguard 66: *Napoleon's Guns 1792–1815 (1) Field Artillery*, Osprey, Oxford, 2003). The height of its wheels was 4ft 10in. (157cm). An identical limber was used for the 16-pdr and 24-pdr guns and the 8-inch howitzer (see Plate B for further details).

Siege trains were much slower to travel than field artillery and the heavy shot and bombs would be carried in whatever appropriate transport there was available. Ideally, the wagons, or 'chariots', used to carry guns were 11ft (3.37m) long by 4ft 4in. and 6 lines (1.47m) wide, those for ammunition and tools 11ft 4in. (3.68m) long. If they belonged to the army, they were painted with two coats of olive-green paint and covered with a canvas roof, though these details could vary a great deal in the field.

Carriages for 16- and 24-pdrs and 8-inch howitzers were each pulled by four horses. The heavy guns transported in wagons needed extra power: a 24-pdr wagon had to be pulled by ten horses, a 16-pdr by eight horses. Two howitzers would fit into a wagon pulled by four horses. Mortars and mortar beds as

Sketch of crude but sturdy gun carriages made in Spain for the French artillery as observed by Col. Alexander Dickson at Olivença in April 1811. 'A' indicates the 'Cheeks added and bolted to Sides of Car'; 'B' shows a 'Block Bolted to pole to diminish the Shock on Firing'. The carriages were pulled by bullocks. (J. H. Leslie, ed., *The Dickson Manuscripts*, Vol. 3, 1811, Woolwich, 1908)

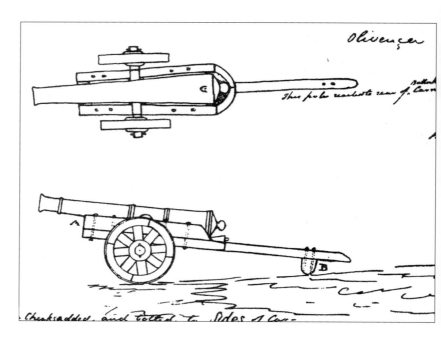

Gribeauval siege guns of the Napoleonic era. In the right foreground, just behind the gunner, is a brass siege 24-pdr on its carriage. Note the little wooden 'roof' to protect the vent. To the left a brass 8-inch siege howitzer on its carriage. The gunners wear the 1812 artillery uniform, but with the white cockade and shako plate with the royal coat of arms worn from 1815. (Print after Moltzheim. Anne S.K. Brown Military Collection, Brown University, USA. Photo RC)

well as most other types of ordnance were each allotted a wagon pulled by four horses, except for the four-wheeled field forges that needed six horses.

An army with a large train of siege artillery would thus require a large number of men, horses and wagons. For instance, an army with 150 siege guns, howitzers and mortars needed 1,142 wagons and 5,624 horses, according to General Gassendi. Of these, some 768 were used to carry cannonballs, ammunition and tools, including four field forges. To conduct all this, a train company was required for every 100 horses, and 51 companies of foot artillery were necessary to serve the guns. This, added to the field artillery and the cartage required for food, gives an idea of what was involved when Napoleon's Grande Armée moved around the Continent.

In Spain and Portugal, some home-made non-regulation carriages were made by the French to cope with the Peninsula's poor roads, difficult terrain and age-old custom of moving anything bulky on primitive but solid carts pulled by slow-moving bullocks. According to Col. Alexander Dickson, who served with the Anglo-Portuguese artillery, the French used a simple but very sturdy 'car' that was pulled by bullocks. Although smaller calibres, up to and including 12-pdrs, were seen by Dickson at Olivenza in April 1811, he felt that these primitive-looking carriages 'would have stood a 16- or 18-pdr, but certainly not beyond that'. A bigger carriage would obviously be needed for larger calibres. The wood used to make these carriages 'was strong and well chosen'. There was a great deal of diversity in the design of these locally made carriages with 'many of much stronger construction than others'. Dickson made a sketch (see opposite) showing a strongly made carriage of basic design with no frills. Two rather surprising features of these carriages were the quoin (or elevation block) rather than the screw and the presence of a block bolted on the pole of the trail to reduce the shock on firing.

Garrison carriages

The garrison carriages (*affûts de place*) were completely redesigned under the Gribeauval system. Previously, the gun crew had to manoeuvre

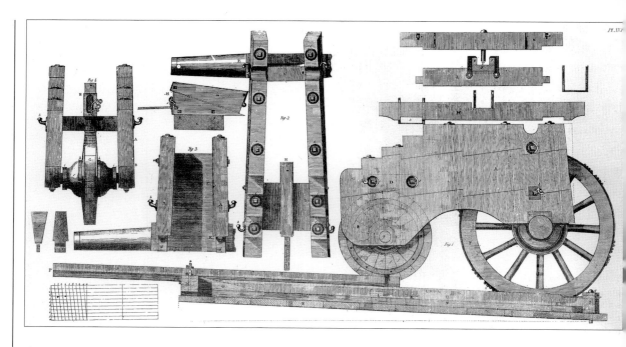

Plan of the profile, top and rear of a Gribeauval garrison carriage for a 16-pdr and its platform. (Print after de Scheel)

the carriage by hand, often causing it to crack or collapse under the stress. Once in position, the gun had to be aimed, something next to impossible to perform at night, before being levered again into place by up to a dozen men. Furthermore, aiming through an embrasure that had to be high enough to protect the gunners provided a limited field of fire. All these strictures ensured that these weapons were rarely effective, even in the best conditions.

Gribeauval had observed the problems with garrison artillery and, as early as 1748, had invented a simple yet novel way to deal with the problem of aiming the gun and speeding up the rate of fire. His solution called for elevated wooden rails upon which a garrison carriage and its gun would be mounted. The part of the carriage supporting the gun was patterned after naval carriages but with somewhat higher cheeks and no small wheels. Instead, two large wheels were fitted at the front and a smaller third wheel at the rear. By carrying its weight on three wheels, it was much more stable, and therefore more accurate. The three wheels ran into three groves made of wooden rails. Set at an angle, the rails allowed the gun to recoil whilst keeping it pointed in the same general direction. When the gun was fired, it would recoil along these rails and be easily and quickly slid up to its aimed firing position again within minutes, thus increasing the defender's rate of fire. This also allowed a garrison to fire at night against enemy siege works with a reasonable degree of accuracy, something that made the repair of works destroyed during the day more difficult and dangerous.

The Gribeauval garrison carriages raised a gun by over two metres from the ground compared to about 130cm for the old wheeled garrison carriages and 65cm for the old naval carriages. High embrasures were not required for the pieces of the new system, 35 to 50cm was enough. This meant that a battery could be set up quickly as the construction of flat firing platforms and high parapets was no longer required. As the wheels were lower than ordinary garrison carriages, their chance of being damaged was

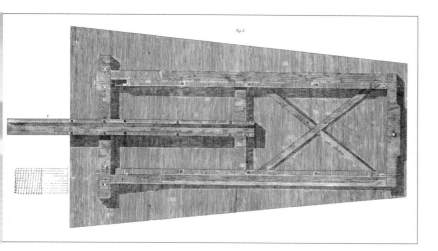

Top view of the garrison carriage platform and rails, two at each side for the front wheels and the central rail for the back wheel. (Print after de Scheel)

lessened, and the gun generally was less exposed than previously. The use of wood as the basis for these carriages also meant they were cheap to build and easy to repair.

Another important feature of the new system was that only five men were needed to serve a gun on a Gribeauval garrison carriage. Except for those employed with sponge and rammer at the gun's muzzle, the gunners were almost invisible from the enemy, with only their arms occasionally exposed rather than their whole body as was previously the case.

Although not a rich man, Gribeauval had a carriage built to test his concept. The results were conclusive and Gribeauval submitted his proposal for a new style of garrison carriage in September 1748. The idea gained support and was passed on to Vallière. He too was enthusiastic and ordered that some of these new garrison carriages be built and tested at Douai. In February 1749, the tests were carried out and the results confirmed the success of Gribeauval's system. Vallière then submitted the new concept to the Master General of Artillery, the Count d'Eu, whilst King Louis XV rewarded Gribeauval for his inspiration. Then, in spite of all these fine opinions, recommendations and approvals, nothing further was done!

Side view of a brass 16-pdr mounted on the Gribeauval garrison carriage and platform. The gunner wears the 1775 uniform but the carriage was the same throughout the Napoleonic Wars. (Print after Moltzheim. Anne S.K. Brown Military Collection, Brown University, USA. Photo RC)

This new design of garrison carriage was not actively promoted in the French artillery for many years thereafter. It was simply filed away probably partly due to the expense and partly due to political infighting at the French court. When Gribeauval was in Austrian service during the Seven Years War, he had guns at Schweidnitz mounted on carriages according to his design and they rendered outstanding service during the city's siege by the Prussians in 1762. This type of carriage was tested again during the 1764 trials at Strasbourg and approved within the new artillery system the following year. Gribeauval eventually became First Inspector-General of Artillery under Louis XVI and, after solving the more pressing issues to do with the field artillery, turned his attention to heavy artillery in the 1770s and 1780s. His style of garrison carriage gradually became more common in fortresses from the 1780s onwards.

Rear view of a Gribeauval garrison carriage and platform dating from 1806. (Print after Marbot. Anne S.K. Brown Military Collection, Brown University, USA. Photo RC)

The basic dimensions of the garrison carriages were:

FOR A 16-PDR GUN

Length of carriage cheeks: 6ft 6in.
Height of carriage cheeks: 2ft 10in.
Front wheels: 4ft 4in.
Small rear wheel: 2ft 8in.
Rail length: 11ft 8in.

FOR A 12-PDR GUN

Length of carriage cheeks: 6ft
Height of carriage cheeks: 2ft 10in.
Front wheels: 4ft 4in.
Small rear wheel: 2ft 8in.
Rail length: 11ft 4in.

FOR AN 8-PDR GUN

Length of carriage cheeks: 5ft 8in.
Height of carriage cheeks: 2ft 10in.
Front wheels: 4ft 4in.
Small rear wheel: 2ft 8in.
Rail length: 11ft

Mortar beds were made of pieces of cast iron bolted together. Wood strengthened with iron had been used until the 1740s, but they proved to be both expensive to make and quick to fail and were replaced by wrought iron beds. The wrought iron beds were more solid and lasted longer but were very heavy. These were replaced again by cast iron and wood beds from the 1760s. Those used in Napoleon's time only had the cheeks (sides) made out of cast iron joined to wooden transoms and fastened with long steel bolts. This mixture of iron with wood made for a solid yet relatively lightweight bed.

Paint and trim

The colour of paint and trim for the carriages and equipment of Napoleon's heavy artillery was generally the same as for the field artillery: the wood was painted olive-green and the ironwork black. The calibre of the gun tended to be indicated in white paint on the upper part of a carriage's cheeks. Details of paint recipes are given in New Vanguard 66: *Napoleon's Guns 1792–1815 (1) Field Artillery* (Osprey, Oxford, 2003). Mortar beds appear to have had either their metal parts in black with olive-green wooden transoms, or entirely painted in black.

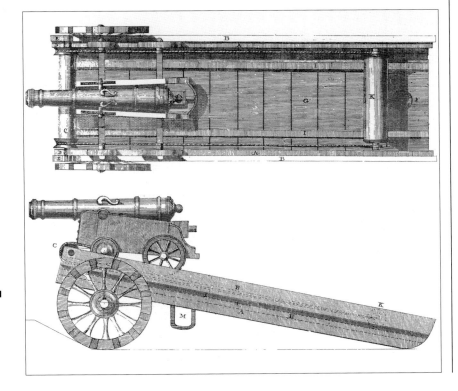

A machine designed to fire over the parapet of a covered way. Cornelius Redlichkeit published details of his invention at The Hague in 1775. It was designed so that besiegers could roll 3-, 4-, 6- and 8-pdrs up in a covered way fairly close to the enemy's walls and fire them in relative safety by a weight and pulley system. Whether it was widely used is unknown. (Print after de Scheel)

SIEGE OPERATIONS

The Gribeauval system siege artillery first saw action in the United States during the American War of Independence. In 1780 the artillery train sent with General Rochambeau's French expeditionary corps featured the new guns. They were under the command of Lt-Col d'Aboville of the Auxonne Regiment, *Corps Royal de l'Artillerie*, whose 2nd battalion served the guns. They landed in Newport, Rhode Island, in the summer of 1780, and the field pieces accompanied the French army as it marched towards Yorktown, Virginia, in 1781. The siege artillery, consisting of 12 24-pdrs, eight 16-pdrs, two 8-inch howitzers and a dozen 8- and 12-inch mortars, remained in Newport until the late summer of 1781, when it was loaded on board the French fleet and was finally landed at Treeball's Landing on the James River on 30 September. Although only 11km from Yorktown, there were not enough horses to pull the artillery train, and 16 bullocks were pressed into service. Several batteries were constructed on the first parallel from 8 October and, from 13 October, the guns were moved into the newly built batteries of the second parallel. These heavy batteries bombarded Yorktown until it surrendered on 19 October. The French eventually re-embarked their siege artillery and sent it the West Indies the following year. On the whole, they were very pleased with the new materiel and few corrections seemed necessary. Twenty years later, Lord Cornwallis confided to d'Aboville that 'it was to you that I should have surrendered since it is your well aimed guns that destroyed all my fortifications'.[2]

The heavy artillery was also deployed with the French armies across Europe during the wars of the French Revolution and Empire, always ready to be brought up to pound an enemy fortress into submission. The guns proved to be remarkably sturdy and easy to serve, even under difficult campaign conditions.

One of the first large sieges of the Revolutionary and Napoleonic wars was that of the port city of Toulon in 1793. It was occupied by British, Spanish and Piedmontese, as well as French royalist troops, but, by September 1793, was surrounded by large numbers of French republican forces. This disorganised revolutionary army included a newly promoted artillery battalion commander, Napoleon Bonaparte. The siege dragged on, and, finally, Bonaparte's ideas on how to take the city were tried out. According to Napoleon, the key was to occupy the peninsula to the south of the city. With

Napoleon proposed a strategy reliant on the use of siege artillery to overcome the British and Spanish at the siege of Toulon in 1793. The Republican commissioners agreed and the city's defenders were driven out. (Print after Raffet)

2 This occurred when the two met during the negotiations leading to the 1802 Treaty of Amiens. Lord Cornwallis was part of the British delegation and d'Aboville, who had risen to general, was part of the French delegation. F. Buttner, 'Les Artilleurs de M. de Rochambeau', *La Sabretache*, numéro spécial, 1976, p. 135.

To galvanise his gunners at the siege of Toulon, Napoleon Bonaparte, who commanded the artillery, asked a young corporal by the name of Andoche Junot (the future senior general) to put up a sign with '*Batterie des hommes sans peur*' (Battery of the fearless men) in front of his gun's position. Thereafter every gunner in the army wished to serve there. This incident shows how Napoleon understood the motivations of men at war and their desire to surpass themselves when well led. (Print after Raffet)

heavy artillery mounted there, the harbour would quickly become untenable, and the enemy fleet would have to withdraw. Methodically, the forts in that area were bombarded by the republicans' heavy artillery siege batteries, then stormed by waves of troops. Bonaparte charged with his men and took a bayonet thrust in the thigh as the British artillery platforms were taken. With the fall of these forts, admirals Hood and Gravina, respectively in command of the British and Spanish contingents, knew the game was up. The only thing to do was to evacuate the city and set fire to the French ships and shore installations as quickly as possible. On the morning of 20 December, the French Republican troops marched into Toulon.

It was Napoleon's baptism of fire, during which he also suffered his first wound. Like the few wounds to follow in his later campaigns, this was a slight one. Toulon was also Napoleon's first taste of glory. He had come up with the successful plan, both strategically and tactically, and delivered Toulon to the Republican Army. His outstanding conduct was rewarded. He was promoted to the rank of Brigadier-General, and Sergeant Andoche Junot, whom Napoleon had met and valued highly during the siege, was commissioned and became his aide-de-camp.

Napoleon's involvement with artillery in his later campaigns was largely restricted to the field artillery. However, the siege and garrison artillery also played an important role, especially in Spain and Portugal between 1808 and 1814. Sieges of cities such as Zaragoza, Gerona, Cadiz, Ciudad Rodrigo, Almeida, Taragona and other towns required large trains of heavy artillery that were, generally speaking, expertly served by the French gunners and officers, all of whom were well trained for the task. In spite of the heroism of the Spanish and Portuguese defenders, the French siege artillery nearly always prevailed. Conversely, the French gunners could prove to be very thorough defenders when besieged, as their outstanding resistance at Badajoz and San Sebastian showed. In France itself, coastal artillery was also used to keep the blockading British ships at a respectable distance.

Often overlooked by historians are the French artillerymen who served their guns in the French colonies in America, Africa and Asia. Relatively few in number and serving old iron naval guns to defend their forts against the far stronger forces of the British and their allies, they nevertheless gave a fine account of themselves at such places as Guadeloupe and Mauritius.

COASTAL ARTILLERY

Coast guard artillery corps

From the Middle Ages, the villages and towns along the French coastline had temporary units that became known as the coast guard militia during the 17th century. This outfit consisted of villagers mustered into units to keep watch and go after raiders who preyed on the coastline. In the 18th century, the organisation and training was formalised so that, by the early 1760s, 40,000 men aged 16 to 60 were on the rolls of this militia, a figure that included every able-bodied man within *c*. 20km from the coast. Further developments led to the establishment of companies of picked men and volunteers who were armed, and even issued uniforms. They would reg-ularly drill and stand watch. This last aspect became increasingly important as more and more small coastal batteries were built at strate-gically important locations. Indeed, up to the 1960s, one could often see ruins of 18th-century coast guard batteries on the northwestern coast of France, generally situated near to concrete bunkers built by the Germans during the Second World War. The 18th-century proliferation of shore batteries greatly increased the number of guns deployed on the coast and required the transformation of an increasing number of coast guard militiamen from infantrymen into artillerymen. As early as 1747, detailed printed regulations for the service and care of coast batteries were distributed.

French siege artillery bombards the fortress town of Luxembourg in 1795. (Print after Renoux)

In 1772, all the infantry companies were transformed into 586 com-panies of coastal artillery and, shortly after the war broke out against Britain in 1778, the whole service was reorganised into a corps of *Canonniers Gardes-Côtes* (coast guard artillerymen) of 418 companies divided into 102 command divisions. During time of war, half of these men were mobilised to serve the batteries, replaced by the other half after a fixed period of time. This system proved quite efficient during the American War of Independence. During a period of peace, all the men assembled for occasional parades and gunnery training. Their cadres were on permanent duty, standing guard over the batteries and keeping the guns and their carriages in serviceable condition.

Following the outbreak of the French Revolution in July 1789, the old and despised royal militia was abolished. The more popular coast guard artillery was also disbanded by a decree of 4 March 1791. It was actually retained for a while by worried coastal inhabitants before being swept away by another order of 9 September 1792. The national guards were supposed to assume this duty but it soon proved to be too much for them. When war broke out with Great Britain (and most of Europe) in early 1793 the coastal batteries were abandoned, leaving many areas of the coast vulnerable to attack. The governing Committee of Public Safety ordered the formation of companies of volunteer gunners at the most exposed points of the coast, and there were soon about 100 companies mustering some 10,000 men mobilised or on stand-by. Although these men were included in the rolls of the national guards they were really coastal artillerymen. A few of these companies may have served with field armies; in 1793–94 the 2nd company of Lyonne is known to have campaigned in Flanders. On 10 September 1799, some 130 companies of volunteer coast guard artillery were to be raised to serve with three battalions of coast guard grenadiers but this sketchy organisation was disbanded on 16 June 1802, except for four drafted battalions that were sent to fight Toussaint L'Ouverture as field artillery in Haiti.

On the whole, the service of the coastal artillery was hampered by an overcomplicated structure until the early 1800s. Once Napoleon came to power as First Consul, the coast guard artillery was reformed by a decree of 28 May 1803, its whole organisation was streamlined and made more intelligible. The coastal batteries were to be refurbished and manned by 100 companies of 119 NCOs and gunners, each led by a captain and a lieutenant. The initial establishment was 220 officers and 11,900 enlisted men. They were drafted from coastal residents between the ages of 25 and 45, with a marked preference shown for retired soldiers. They were liable for service in the batteries up to age of 50. This was not considered to be a hardship as it ensured that most men from the coastal villages and towns would not be conscripted into the Grande Armée. These companies were assisted by 28 companies of auxiliary sedentary gunners who acted as a reserve. For every ten companies or more, there was a small cadre of permanent staff officers for that '*direction*' (roughly a district) responsible for administration. In December 1808, each *direction* became an administrative council with increased powers over training and discipline. Each council had a director who was a field grade officer, a 'coast adjutant', the senior artillery captain and a senior NCO, who acted as secretary. They arranged the gunnery training and would sometimes turn up at batteries unannounced for surprise inspections.

Coast guard artillerymen normally served in batteries near their homes. They only served 50 per cent of the time, being on duty at the batteries for four days and off duty for four days at a time in normal circumstances. They were drafted for a service of five years in full time or ten years in half time. Theirs was largely a preventive duty. They watched for enemy ships and corsairs, mostly British, who occasionally staged raids on the French coast. Most actions were limited to firing off a few rounds at ships that got too close. However, there were times when enemy landing parties attempted to take an isolated battery and fighting

French artillery on the march in the early 1800s. The crews of the artillery train could pull the lower calibres of siege artillery. (Print after Raffet)

would occur. In such cases, the alarm would be raised and troops would soon converge on the threatened area.

After ten years of service, the men drafted into the corps were released from duty. The uniform issued was to last five to ten years and could be kept by the coast guard artillerymen after their release. The men's portable weapons were carried only on service, otherwise they were to be kept at the nearest town hall.

As time passed, the extent of the French empire grew as Belgium, Holland and parts of Italy were absorbed into France, the number of companies rose and by 1811 the force stood at 140 companies totalling about 17,300 officers and men. Of these, about half actually served in the batteries rotating in four-day shifts. At that time, Napoleon must have wondered about the effectiveness of having some 8,500 gunners deployed in coastal batteries for a generally quiet and sedentary duty,. especially as there were widespread rumours that some turned a blind eye to smugglers from Britain. Napoleon was particularly interested in the companies serving on the French and Belgian coast along the English Channel. He inspected these troops and their batteries personally in 1803 and 1811. He also ordered a study to explore alternative ways to organise these units such as grouping some into field regiments to serve with the land armies. However, this proved to be impractical, as the coastline still had a need for troops to protect it. Napoleon finally decided to maintain the coast guard artillery as it was and nothing much was done to change its basic organisation.

At times, some coast guard artillerymen were drafted into companies organised for naval or colonial service. After the disastrous French invasion of Russia in 1812, Napoleon mobilised the coast guard artillery units for full time duty. First the companies posted from the Channel to the Baltic in late 1812, and from early 1813 the units from the Atlantic to the Adriatic. By then, the Allies were gaining ground and closing in on France itself. A

A 48-pdr iron naval gun. These very large guns were made at the end of the 17th century. When they were found to be too heavy for warships, some were mounted in batteries to defend naval bases, notably at Brest. These were probably the largest coastal artillery pieces at the time. (Archives Nationales, Marine, G203)

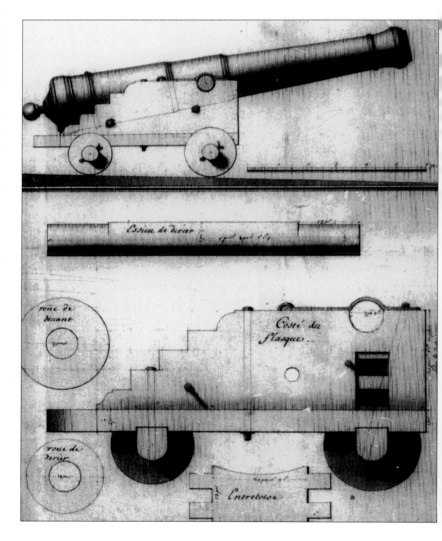

'MARINE' (Navy) etched at the rear of a model 1721 iron naval gun. (Photo RC)

Coastal artillery guns mounted on the later pattern of Gribeauval traversing platforms in the1790s. The guns shown appear to be old land artillery pieces. (Print by A. Raffet)

number of the mobilised coast guard artillerymen were formed into 27 mobile companies on 22 January 1814. These were attached to each of the regiments of regular artillery as the 29th, 30th and 31st companies. They thus served in the Campaign of France. The rest remained at their local batteries but, by April 1814, much of the French coast had come under the control of the Allies and the French royalists and the coast guard artillery was disbanded on 20 April by the royalist government.

When Napoleon came back to France for his last 'Hundred Days' of imperial government in 1815, he ordered 80 companies of coast guard artillery raised again on 24 April. The organisation was probably only partly completed by the time the battle of Waterloo was fought on 18 June. Following the second and final exile of Napoleon and the return of King Louis XVIII to power, the coast guard artillery was permanently disbanded on 14 August 1815.

Coastal artillery naval ordnance

As noted above, the guns and mortars served by coast guard artillerymen in the batteries were overwhelmingly iron naval ordnance models. It should be stressed here that there were a substantial number of guns in the coastal forts and batteries during Napoleon's reign. It is estimated that about 3,000 pieces of artillery were mounted and kept in working order by the coast guard artillerymen until 1815.

These guns were basically of two types: older guns that might no longer be suitable at sea but equal to coastal battery duty; and new guns that were of good quality except that they were somewhat too heavy to be ideally suited for use at sea. These guns, when well looked after, were perfectly suitable for coastal artillery. Some older land service guns might also occasionally be found in coastal batteries but, as a rule, both the guns and their carriages were of naval patterns.

In the Peninsula, French ordnance captured by Wellington's army revealed a varied mixture of guns. By late 1813, as Wellington's army neared France, naval guns were increasingly present in the French Army's arsenal. At the passage of the Bidossa on 7 October 1813, four iron 24-pdrs on travelling carriages and eight iron 8-pdrs on naval carriages were reported taken. These were obviously naval iron guns, the 24-pdrs pressed into service as siege artillery and most likely mounted on the large Gribeauval siege carriages, the 8-pdrs were simply used as garrison guns much like those in coastal forts. A month later, on 10 November 1813, Wellington's army was at the French border and crossed into France at Saint-Jean-de-Luz. There, it found in its 'very strong' works, besides six brass field guns, some 52 iron guns 'mounted on Garrison [or naval] Carriages' namely:

10	24-pdrs
6	18-pdrs
7	8-pdrs
13	6-pdrs
16	4-pdrs

These guns, Lt. Col. Alexander Dickson reported, were turned on the retreating French columns by the Portuguese artillerymen. The French gunners had spiked some but obviously not most of them.

In France, unlike Great Britain, land and naval ordnance services were two separate entities. Until 1859, the Board of Ordnance procured designs for both the army and the Royal Navy in Britain. In France the army and the navy were governed by two separate and powerful ministries. Everything covered so far in this study was procured by the Ministry of War, the department responsible for the army. The Gribeauval and Year XI artillery systems were designed for the army's artillery services by officers who belonged to the army's artillery corps. Although this is much less known, the Ministry of the Navy was responsible for the design and production of the ordnance pertaining to ships of war. As the Ministry of the Navy was responsible for the administration of French colonies and also had a role in France's coastal defences, a sizeable part of Napoleon's guns were naval guns.

Naval artillery covered the whole range of calibres from 4-pdrs through to 36-pdrs and 48-pdrs from the 1690s that were found to be too heavy for ships. The calibres in use from the 1690s to 1820 were: 4-pdr, 6-pdr, 8-pdr, 12-pdr, 18-pdr, 24-pdr and 36-pdr. The reason for their heavy weight was that naval guns were nearly all made of iron. Out of 7,774 guns belonging to the navy in 1768, only 186 were made of brass and all the rest of iron.[3] By 1790, there were 8,728. Three years later, the Revolutionary Government felt 6,000 more were needed to arm a fleet of 100 ships-of-the-line and 160 frigates. Such figures were never reached but gun production remained high, especially during the period 1807–13 when Napoleon was trying to rebuild the fleet.

New guns were meant for warships. However, those of the new guns that were found to be too heavy were rejected for ships and, if they passed the proofing trials, were used in the coastal batteries and fortifications guarding seaports. Such guns were also sent to be placed in forts defending the French colonies. This was also the case for older guns judged too hazardous for service at sea but good enough to arm batteries in France or overseas.

The lengths and weights varied from those given below. Lengths, especially before 1786, could vary by two or three centimetres. The weights could vary much more. A batch of 28 iron 36-pdrs guns cast at Indret in 1782 had an average weight of 3,906kg but individual guns varied from 3,677kg to 4,057kg. Technical improvements in casting reduced these differences later on.

3 The navy's brass guns were cast at government foundries located at Rochefort and Toulon, set up in 1669 and 1667 respectively. The Toulon foundry closed in the early-19th century while the operations of the Rochefort foundry were transferred to Ruelle in 1840. Although the heavy guns were nearly all of iron, the foundries still cast brass swivel guns as well as the many brass items needed on ships. The navy's brass was made the same way as the army's: 90 per cent copper mixed with 10 per cent pewter.

Senior gunner, coast guard artillery, 1803–10. This plate by JOB (Jacques Onfroy de Bréville) is after a coloured sketch by B. de Valmont, a French naval officer during the first third of the 19th century. It shows the coast guard artilleryman wearing the white faced with blue uniform ordered on 1 September 1803. Except for the cuff flaps, which are blue instead of red, this uniform matches the specification. As the uniforms were to last five years or more, a good many coast guard artillerymen continued to wear the blue and green uniform.

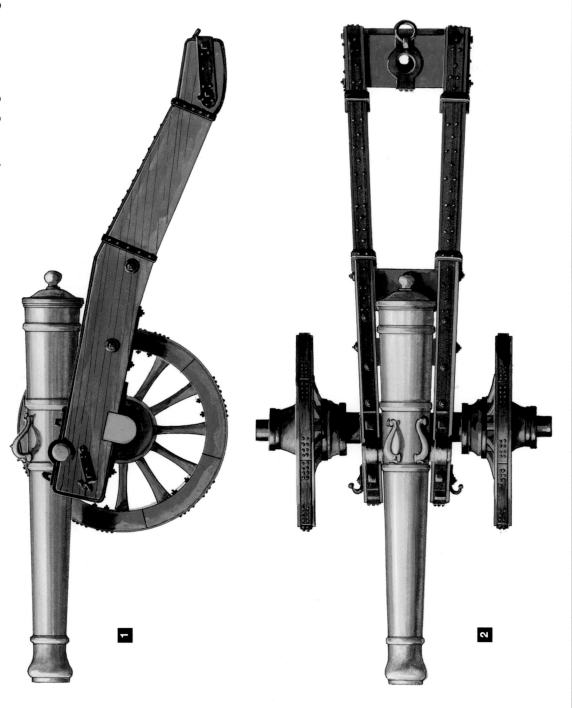

A: Gribeauval brass 24-pdr siege gun and carriage

1

2

A

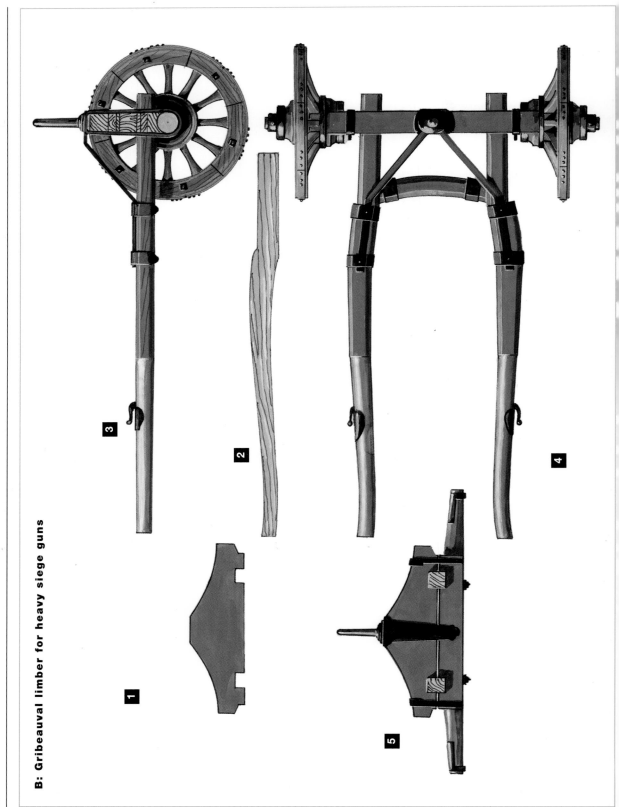

B: Gribeauval limber for heavy siege guns

C: Gribeauval coastal artillery traversing platform

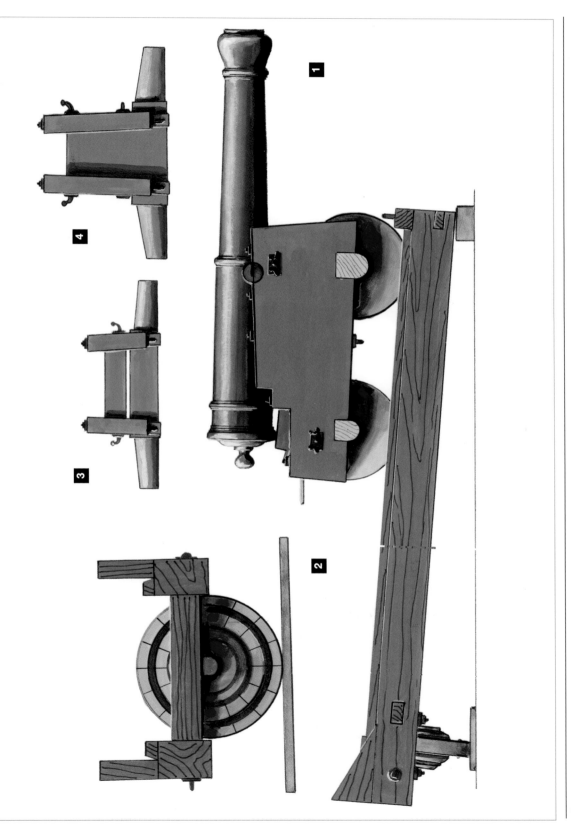

D: COASTAL ARTILLERY NAVAL IRON 36-PDR GUN ON A GRIBEAUVAL TRAVERSING PLATFORM

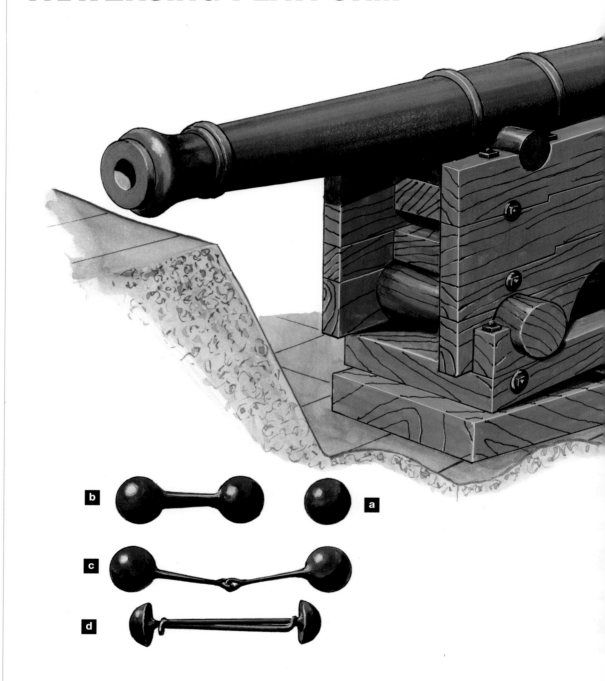

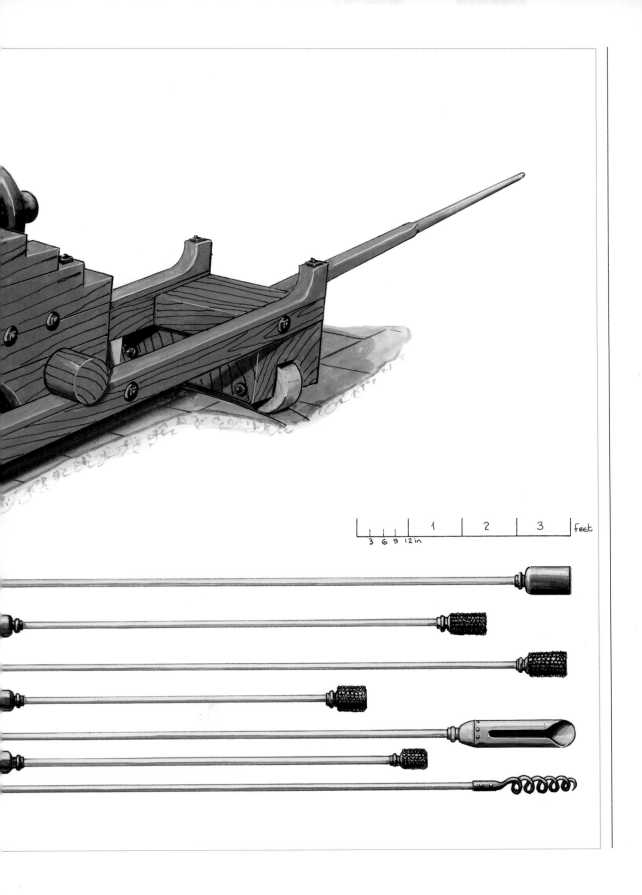

3 6 9 12in   1   2   3   feet

E: Gribeauval garrison carriage for a brass 16-pdr

F: Mortars and mortar bombs

1

2

3

4

5

6

7

8

1 2 3   6   9   12
inches

G: 10-inch Gribeauval mortar with its bed

The design of naval artillery pieces changed several times in the 18th century. In 1721, guns were approved that remained in use with some variations until 1766, when naval guns were reduced in length and weight. Although the regulation ordering this was issued in 1767, the new models were approved the previous year and are known as the 1766 model guns. These were as follows:

Bombardment of Ancona by the Russo-Turkish fleet in 1799. From 16 May, General Monnier and a garrison of some 2,500 French and Italian troops resisted for months against vastly superior numbers of Russian, Turkish and Austrian forces. Monnier and his men finally capitulated on 16 November. The siege featured many artillery duels between the town's batteries and the allied fleet in which the French gunners prevailed, in spite of using older types of guns and carriages. (Print after Martinet)

CALIBRE	LENGTH	WEIGHT
36-pdr	2,880mm	3,646kg
24-pdr	2,729mm	2,593kg
18-pdr	2,560mm	2,104kg
12-pdr	2,400mm	1,590kg
8-pdr	2,190mm	1,101kg
6-pdr	2,020mm	832kg
4-pdr	1,760mm	563kg

Despite the shortening of the guns in the 1766 regulation, many officers still considered them too long and they were changed again in 1778 according to a regulation issued in 1779. For frigates being built at Saint-Malo, some of the smaller calibre guns were made to a short pattern. The 1778 models were:

CALIBRE	LENGTH	WEIGHT
36-pdr	2,870mm	3,866kg
24-pdr	2,729mm	2,593kg
18-pdr	2,492mm	2,250kg
12-pdr	2,413mm	1,663kg
12-pdr (short)	2,176mm	
8-pdr	2,190mm	1,223kg
8-pdr (short)	1,920mm	1,089kg
6-pdr	2,015mm	889kg
6-pdr (short)	1,740mm	795kg
4-pdr	1,750mm	
4-pdr (short)	1,530mm	465kg

The 1778 models did not prove very satisfactory for arming ships as they were found to be too heavy. Their manufacture was stopped in 1783 and foundries were instructed to revert to casting the 1766 models. This, however, was not done everywhere as 1778 model guns were cast at Indret in 1785. Three years later, the new Inspector-General of the *Corps Royal de l'Artillerie des Colonies* (Royal Corps of Colonial Artillery), General de Manson, was asked to design a new system of naval ordnance. Manson, a close colleague of Gribeauval, was familiar with all aspects of ordnance design and came up with a successful system that lasted until 1820. It was officially brought in by a royal order of 26 October 1786. The 1786 model guns were lighter and featured a much cleaner design than the 1778 models, with mouldings either eliminated or simplified. The vent astragal, the rounded moulding that circled the barrel closest to the vent near the breech, was initially removed, but later reinstated. The astragal at the base of the swell was removed on lighter calibres and replaced by a plain ring on 18-, 24- and 36-pdrs. The trunnions on all the guns were reinforced by a rimbase. The 6- and 8-pdr long guns were introduced to improve long range firing. These 1786 models, the main type of naval gun used during the Napoleonic period, were as follows:

Coast guard militia dragoon, artilleryman and infantryman lounging around a brass mortar in a coastal battery, c. 1770. As the coastal militia was increasingly devoted to serving guns, it was transformed into the coast guard artillery corps in 1778. (Print after Marbot. Anne S.K. Brown Military Collection, Brown University, USA. Photo RC)

CALIBRE	LENGTH	WEIGHT
36-pdr	2,865mm	3,520kg
24-pdr	2,735mm	2,500kg
18-pdr	2,572mm	2,060kg
12-pdr	2,430mm	1,470kg
8-pdr	2,598mm	1,170kg
8-pdr (short)	2,219mm	1,005kg
6-pdr	2,273mm	840kg
6-pdr (short)	2,003mm	630kg
4-pdr	1,792mm	540kg
4-pdr (short)	1,538 mm	390kg

(Note: the iron naval 4-pdr was abandoned in 1786 but reintroduced in 1787.)

The long 4-, 6- and 8-pdrs were designed to be mounted on the quarter-decks where their length enabled them to clear the rigging and provide oblique fire.

Coastal artillery 36-pdr iron model 1778 naval gun mounted on a traversing carriage, 1780s. The gun is slid back and being loaded. Two gunners ram in the charge while another plugs the vent.

The 1786 model naval guns proved to be an excellent design and remained the regulation system during the Napoleonic Wars with hardly any changes. The only notable alteration came around 1810 when a small patch was added parallel to the vent to provide better support for the gunlocks. Only from 1820 were new models of ordnance introduced in

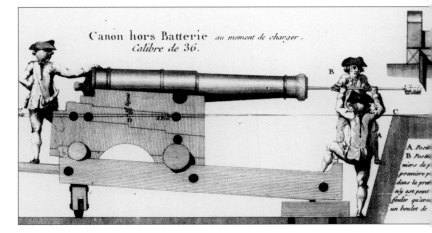

Canon hors Batterie au moment de charger.
Calibre de 36.

A Partie
B Partie
mière de p
premiere
dans la prat
n'y est point
fouler qu'avec
un boulet de

the French navy. The number of men needed to serve each calibre of gun was as follows:

CALIBRE	CHIEF	SERVANTS	PURVEYOR	TOTAL
36-pdr	1	12	1	14
24-pdr	1	10	1	12
18-pdr	1	8	1	10
12-pdr	1	8	1	10
8-pdr	1	6	1	8
6-pdr	1	4	1	6
4-pdr	1	4	1	6

This was for guns on ships and on ordinary platforms in batteries. The number of crew could be cut by half if Gribeauval's carriages were installed in the batteries.

Each gun was to have 70 rounds, ten of which were to be bar shot. In 1804, the quantity of powder for each shot was, according to calibre: 36-pdr = 12lb; 24-pdr = 8lb; 18-pdr = 6lb; 12-pdr = 4lb; 8-pdr = $2\,^2/_3$lb; 6-pdr = 2lb; 4-pdr = $1\,^1/_3$lb.

Naval mortars

The design of mortars in the French navy at the time of Napoleon was not standardised and would not be until 1840. As the navy did not need as many mortars as the army, and the ideal design was uncertain, the designs were left to vary with almost every batch of mortars to be cast.

Some naval mortars were intended to serve on bomb ketches, but most were to be found within coastal batteries. From the mid-18th century, naval mortars intended to be installed in forts were cast of iron and, by the late-1790s, a 12-inch iron Gomer chamber mortar type specifically designed for the coastal artillery was cast. Prior to this point naval mortars were traditionally made of brass.

From the late-17th century, the calibre of most French naval mortars was 12-inch although some 9-, 8- and 7-inch mortars were also produced. Naval mortars either had trunnions to be mounted on mortar beds or were cast complete with a large base plate and would be fastened to a large wooden block bed.

As with land mortars the chamber designs of naval mortars saw several variations such as the spherical and cylindrical inner chambers. The same problems regarding flow of gases on ignition that quickly rendered a mortar unserviceable were encountered in the navy as in the army mortars. And, as in the army, the truncated conical chamber invented by Gomer in 1785 was also used. However, naval mortars tended to be fired using a greater charge of powder for maximum range against ships, so whilst naval ordnance officers welcomed Gomer's design they continued to use mortars with pear-

Coastal artillery 36-pdr iron Model 1778 naval gun mounted on a traversing carriage being aimed. The gun is now moved forward. The gunner aiming adjusts the wooden quoin with the help of another gunner handling a lever.

shaped chambers or a combination of both designs. Pear-shaped chambers were easier to reinforce, held more powder and ignited better.

Naval carronades

The French noted with some interest the introduction of carronades in the British Royal Navy from 1779. This new type of gun was effective to a range of 300m against a ship's rigging and crew. However, French marine gunners were not too thrilled at using this weapon as it required them to serve it in the open and at close range. Its rate of fire of about three shots a minute was appreciated, but it was estimated that it could only fire for two hours at that rate while an ordinary naval gun, although it had a slower rate of fire, could last up to eight hours in battle. In 1794, some 24-pdr and 36-pdr carronades were cast in brass for the French navy and put in frigates and smaller vessels. In May 1804, it was decided that carronades would also be used on ships-of-the-line, and that 12- and 18-pdrs would be cast in iron, like the British carronades.

Their general appearance was similar to British carronades and their calibres, lengths and weights were:

Naval 18-pdr iron model 1778 gun. This gun was cast in 1785 at the Indret iron works and marked No. 75. Its companion gun in the background was cast in 1786 and marked No. 130. These guns were preserved at Plymouth, Montserrat, West Indies. (Photo RC)

CALIBRE	LENGTH	WEIGHT
36-pdr	208cm	1,250kg
24-pdr	181cm	850kg
18-pdr	165cm	590kg
12-pdr	143cm	389kg

In practice, 12- and 18-pdr carronades continued to arm French gunboats and smaller craft, whilst the large 24- and 36-pdrs were found on ships-of-the-line. There were also some in coastal forts as three heavy calibre carronades were found by the British in the fortifications at Saint-Jean-de-Luz in November 1813. In general, the French navy was not too keen on carronades and they did not form an important part of its armament.

Garrison and coastal artillery carriages

Up to the last decades of the 18th century, coastal artillery guns were mounted on chariot-style carriages with four small wheels, the same as those used at sea. Carriages rested upon wooden platforms on the ramparts and fired through embrasures in the wall of the fort or coastal battery. To 'follow' a moving ship with such carriages demanded strenuous work by a gun crew equipped with wooden handspikes. Loading was also slow and aiming the gun at such a moving target was equally difficult.

Coast guard artilleryman (left) and a soldier of the Imperial Customs (right), c. 1810. Note the coastal artillery gun on a traversing carriage in the background. (Print after Martinet)

The cheeks of the naval carriages were 1.70m long for 36-pdrs, 1.62m for 24-pdrs, 1.50m for 18-pdrs, 1.46m for 12-pdrs, 1.49m for long 8-pdrs, 1.40m for short 8-pdrs, 1.30m for long 6-pdrs, 1.22m for short 6-pdrs, 1.14m for long 4-pdrs and 1.06m for short 4-pdrs. The cheeks were made of ash and the axles of oak or of elm.

However, as with the garrison artillery, thought had been given to improving the equipment of the coastal artillery. Gribeauval's invention of the garrison platform opened the way to another brilliant innovation: the traversing platform. This was invented by the Sieur Berthelot and it was first built at Auxonne in 1764. This first version was too low and had an excessive amount of ironwork. However, these faults were corrected by Berthelot who raised its height and greatly simplified its construction by eliminating most of the ironwork in the process. Gribeauval was impressed by Berthelot's invention and his coastal artillery carriage with traversing platform was adopted as part of the Gribeauval system in 1765.

The new coastal artillery equipment consisted of a naval-style carriage fitted with wheels (or 'trucks'), somewhat larger than the standard naval carriage wheels, placed on an elevated traversing platform that mounted two long rails. The rails were set at a slight angle raising gradually towards the rear to slow the gun's recoil with the help of gravity. At the rail's front was a pivot pin. At the centre of the rear (or trail) transom was a small wheel that fitted into a semi-circular iron rail (or 'racer') set in the ground. By pushing the back of the rail to the right or left the gun could 'traverse' a wide arc and follow a moving target smoothly with few difficulties, especially if the embrasures were lowered or removed. While it still required a great deal of handling with handspikes and ropes, the traversing carriage made coastal guns much more effective as they could now follow their target much better and fire more quickly.

As the wooden rail extended to some eight feet in length from front to back and swung around when the carriage traversed, these carriages took up a lot of space. The length of the rails appears to have been the same no matter what size carriage (and hence calibre of gun) was used. Enough space had to be left so that the artillerymen serving neighbouring guns would not get in each other's way. It was therefore the usual practice to leave an interval of at least 7m between each position. A coastal battery's concentration of firepower was not affected as all the guns could easily aim and fire at a single ship, while at the same time offering scattered targets over a wide distance to the ship's guns, which could not traverse.

Naturally, this carriage was more expensive than ordinary garrison ones and it was totally unfeasible to mount all the 3,000 guns in the many batteries dotting the coastline. Therefore, many guns remained mounted simply on garrison carriages without the benefit of a traversing platform during the Napoleonic period. The new carriages would usually be installed in major works or in key batteries. The guns mounted on traversing platforms were also more likely to be the heavier 24- and 36-

pdrs that had a longer range and more pounding power. It should also be mentioned that Berthelot's invention certainly did not go unnoticed elsewhere. By the 1790s, other powers, including Britain, had appreciated the impact of this innovative design and were installing traversing carriages based on Gribeauval's design in forts across the world.

Colonial artillery

The French colonies are rarely mentioned in studies on French artillery, yet they all were involved in many actions, against the British in particular, during the wars of the French Revolution and Empire. A typical colonial garrison's artillery would consist of some regular gunners backed up by gunners from the local National Guards (see Men-at-Arms 211: *Napoleon's Overseas Army*, Osprey, Oxford, 1989, for the organisation and uniforms of these troops). On the whole, the ordnance available to colonial gunners was largely similar to what was used by the coastal artillery in France. The majority of pieces were iron naval guns too old or too heavy for sea service. The heavy brass pieces were usually older army models that were transferred overseas during the 18th century. In 1788, Martinique had 26 36-pdrs, 116 24-pdrs, 43 18-pdrs, 25 12-pdrs, 19 12-inch iron mortars, one brass 12-inch mortar and two 10-inch brass mortars. In 1797, the forts and batteries in Guadeloupe had 12 36-pdrs, 73 24-pdrs, 67 18-pdrs, 29 12-pdrs, 31 8-pdrs, 35 6-pdrs, 41 4-pdrs, 6 3-pdrs, 4 2-pdrs, 20 12-inch mortars, two 10-inch mortars, six other mortars of lesser calibres, an 8-inch howitzer and several more of lesser calibres. Shortly before the British attack in 1810, Ile-de-France (Mauritius) had 103 24-pdrs, 56 18-pdrs, 28 12-pdrs, 58 8-pdrs, two 6-pdrs, four 12-inch iron mortars, 14 6-inch iron mortars, two 6-inch brass mortars, and six other mortars in iron or brass.

Portrait of Admiral Bruix, c. 1810. Note the iron mortar and the coastal artillery iron guns on traversing carriages inthe background. (Print after E. Charpentier)

ABOVE **'INDRET'** cast into the left trunnion of a naval 18-pdr iron model 1778 gun cast in 1785. According to the 1767 instructions, this trunnion was to have the initial of the master founder. The foundry at Indret cast its first guns in 1778, became a royal (or government) establishment in 1781 and remained an important gun maker during the Napoleonic era. (Photo RC)

BELOW **Fleur-de-lis** cast into the right trunnion of the naval 18-pdr iron Model 1778 gun. According to the 1767 instructions, it was the foundry's name or marking that was to be cast in the right trunnion. However, the foundry at Indret – which cast this gun between 1781 and 1783 – obviously decided to show the lily on the left trunnion and its name on the right. A good many of Napoleon's naval guns still bore the royal lily. (Photo RC)

Markings and paint

The markings on naval iron guns cast before 1767 were rather erratic. Some had the weight marked on the base ring and sometimes the word 'Marine'. Other marks might be found on one of the trunnion ends, for instance 'IN' for the foundry at Indret or 'RV' for the one at Ruelle. The other trunnion end might have the initials of the founder. These were put on the trunnions so that if the gun exploded when being proofed, the founder who had cast the defective gun could be identified. The markings were usually engraved and rust and corrosion has erased many of them on surviving iron naval guns. Those markings that were moulded in have survived much better.

Markings were not compulsory until an order of 1 January 1767 made them mandatory. This order stipulated that the base ring needed to have the year the gun was cast and the gun number (starting from 1 each year). The right trunnion had to have a letter or sign to identify the foundry, while the left trunnion bore the initial of the master founder. Thus, a gun cast in 1781 had 'RV' for Ruelle on the right trunnion and 'BA' for the founder Baynaud on the left trunnion. The 1767 instructions were modified in 1786 with the year of the casting now on the left side of the base ring and the two initial letters of the contractor on the right side; on the right trunnion the letters identifying the forge, and its weight on the left trunnion. The gun's number, with the letters 'MA' above, was to be carved into the first reinforce to indicate the gun's approval after proofing. The defective, but still serviceable, guns were marked with a 'T'. These were generally used in coastal batteries. At the time of the First Empire, c. 1804–15, all the basic information concerning the gun such as its weight, calibre, number, foundry and year of casting was to be found on the base ring. In practice, as can be seen on actual guns, there were many variations illustrating that the marking instructions were followed rather loosely by foundries and arsenals. A 36-pdr cast at Indret had 'IN' on the right trunnion and 'A 1787 No 48 P 7243' (year 1787, gun No. 48, weight 7,243lb). Indret sometimes used its full name on the trunnions while Liège only used an 'L'. One 36-pdr gun has 'L 187 1809' (Liège, gun No. 187, year 1809) carved into the breech face rather than the base ring. Some arsenals might occasionally carve an anchor design or a peculiar sign or letter not covered in the regulations. Furthermore, the pre-1789 royal foundries also used a fleur-de-lis, possibly carved on the gun or cast in the trunnion. The main foundries casting iron guns for the French navy from the 1780s to the 1820s were Ruelle (along with many smaller neighbouring forges in Périgord), Indret, Nevers, Le Creusot, Saint-Gervais and Liège (from 1803 to 1814)

The naval iron guns were painted with a coat or two of black. A small batch of black paint required 1oz of fine charcoal black, 10oz of yellow ochre,

1lb of linseed oil, 1oz of litharge and $\frac{1}{2}$oz of copperas (ferrous sulphate heptahydrate), these last two ingredients were wrapped in a cloth bag and boiled in the oil for an hour until it became like a syrup. The ochre, charcoal, copperas and litharge were then all mixed together with oil added to the desired consistency.

The wood of the naval carriages on ships were painted red although this gradually changed to yellow ochre during the later part of Napoleon's reign. The iron parts were painted black. On land, the coastal artillery carriages and platforms were painted the same as the army's artillery, with olive-green wood and black iron. The calibre of the gun tended to be indicated in white paint on the upper part of a carriage's cheeks. Of course, there could be variations caused by the finishing of stocks of the light blue/grey paint used by the coastal artillery prior to the Revolution.

Rear view of a French naval 36-pdr iron Model 1786 cannon cast in Liège in 1809. It is marked '187' and '1809'. (Courtesy of Scott Sheads)

AFTERMATH

During the Peninsular War, French gunners were particularly impressed with certain features of the British artillery they saw in Portugal and Spain. The British block trail carriage and its limber with ammunition boxes doubling as seats for gunners raised a great deal of interest. It was impossible to change the system drastically whilst the war still raged on but, after the French were finally defeated at the battle of Waterloo in 1815, the British artillery was the subject of several reports and General Vallée, the new First Inspector General, implemented many changes leading to the replacement of the Gribeauval system. The British-style carriages and limbers were adopted from 1825. The army's guns were finally updated with fine new designs that became known as the Vallée system introduced from 1827. The navy too upgraded its guns from 1830.

GLOSSARY

affût – gun carriage.
avant train – limber.
boutefeu – a linstock or a portfire stick.
bricole – a leather shoulder belt worn by gunners attached to a rope of varying length with a hook at its end.
caisson – ammunition wagon. This term is the standard word in several languages, including English, for denoting such wagons.
canister – a tin cylinder filled with iron balls attached to a *sabot* and powder cartridge bag; fired at close range against charging infantry or cavalry.

A 12-inch iron naval mortar cast in 1772 on a Gribeauval pattern bed. (Fort Ticonderoga. Photo RC)

cap-square – the iron fittings closed over a gun or howitzer's trunnions to secure the barrel onto its carriage.

cascabel – the knob or rose on the end of a gun barrel.

case shot – hollow cast-iron shot with musket balls in the centre; an anti-personnel weapon.

cravat – from the French *Cravatte*, a sort of priming tube made up of two intertwined inflammable cotton cords inserted in a reed. It was inserted in the vent before firings.

écouvillon – sponge. Combined with the ramrod (*refouloir*) from 1801.

écouvillon à manche recourbée – crooked handle sponge.

handspike – a wooden rod that was fitted into the pointing rings at the base of a trail and used to move the piece from side to side.

lanterne – a ladle, made of copper fixed on a rod, combined with a worm after 1801.

limber chest – the ammunition chest, its name derived from the fact that it was usually carried on a limber, although it was also carried on a caisson.

lunette – the iron circle at the rear of a gun's trail that fits into the hook on a limber so it can be pulled.

pointing rings – pairs of parallel iron rings on the carriage's trail. Rods, called pointing handspikes, were slipped into the rings to point the gun. Rods were also inserted in iron handles on top of the carriage of 4-, 6- and 8-pdrs and field artillery howitzers.

priming wire – see vent pick.

prolonge – a rope usually carried twisted on the trail of the gun with a hook at one end to fit into the *lunette* at the rear of a gun's trail, and an iron handle at the other with loops along its length that was used by the gunners to pull a gun off a firing line when hooking it to a limber was impossible.

refouloir – rammer, combined with a sponge (*écouvillon*) from 1801.

sabot – a block of wood fitted at the end of a round.

shell – hollow shot filled with black powder that was fired by howitzers.

solid shot – spherical solid ammunition of cast iron, a cannonball.

thumbstall – a piece of padded leather usually worn on a gunner's left thumb (but also on the index) to cover the vent during cleaning and loading. This was to prevent air causing a draft in the bore that risked igniting any embers or lighted residue left in the chamber. This could cause a premature firing with disastrous consequences for the gunner ramming in the charge.

trunnions – the circular protrusions at the centre of each side of a gun or howitzer. These fitted onto the carriage to hold the barrel.

vent pick – an iron pick, twisted into a circle at one end (or having a wooden handle) and coming to a point at the other used to pierce the powder bag before lighting the Cravat to fire the piece (*dégorgeoir* in French).

windage – space between the diameter of the barrel's bore and the diameter of the cannonball.

worm – an iron corkscrew-shaped instrument fitted to the end of a long wooden pole. It was used to search the bore after firing to remove remaining pieces of smouldering powder bags and embers so as to prevent premature firings (*mèche à vis or tirreboure* in French).

Side view of a French naval 36-pdr iron model 1786 cannon cast in Liège in 1807. (Courtesy of Scott Sheads)

BIBLIOGRAPHY

Blackmore, Howard L., *The Armouries of the Tower of London I Ordnance* (London, 1976). Excellent catalogue featuring many French guns.

Bonnel, Capitaine, *Historique du 2e Régiment d'Artillerie 1720–1898* (Grenoble, 1899)

Boudriot, Jean, 'L'artillerie de mer française, 1674–1856', *Neptunia*, Nos. 89–95 (1968–69)

Correspondence militaire de Napoléon 1er (Paris, 1876), Vol. 7

Corvisier, André, ed., *Dictionnaire d'art et d'histoire militaire* (Paris, 1988)

Fouchy, M. de, *Éloge de M. le marquis de Vallière* (Paris, 1776)

Gassendi, General, *Aide-mémoire à l'usage des officiers d'artillerie de France* (Paris, 1789, 1801), 2 vols. An essential source.

Gooding, S. James, ed., *Elementary Treatise on the Forms of Cannon & Various Systems of Artillery Translated for the use of Cadets of the U.S. Military Academy from the French of Professor N. Persy of Metz 1832* (Bloomfield, 1979). A very valuable overview.

Graves, Donald E., ed., *De Scheel's Treatise on Artillery* (Bloomfield, 1984). An outstanding annotated edition of the 1800 American edition as translated by Col. Jonathan Williams, US Corps of engineers.

Griffith, Patrick, *French Artillery* (London, 1976). Especially valuable on battle manoeuvre and massed firepower.

Hennet, Léon, 'Les milices gardes-côtes', *Revue maritime et coloniale*, Vol. 89 (1887). Coastal artillery troops source.

Hicks, James E., *Notes on French Ordnance* (1938, republished as *French Military Weapons 1777–1938* in 1964).

Lauerma, Matti, *L'artillerie de campagne française pendant les guerres de la Révolution: évolution de l'organisation et de la tactique* (Kerava, Finland, 1956). Excellent on field artillery.

Nardin, Pierre, *Gribeauval: Lieutenant général des armées du roi 1715-1789* (Paris, *c.* 1981). The definitive biography.

Peterson, Harold L., *Round Shot and Rammers* (New York, 1969)

Picard, Ernest, and Louis Jouan, *L'Artillerie française au XVIIIe siècle* (Paris, 1906). An essential source.

Rose, Lester A., *Archeological Metrology: English, French, American and Canadian Systems of Weights and Measures for North American Historical Archeology* (Ottawa, 1983)

Scheel, M. de, *Mémoires d'artillerie, concernant l'artillerie nouvelle, ou les changements faits dans l'artillerie française en 1765* (Copenhagen, 1777; 2nd edition, Paris, 1795). Outstanding work on the Gribeauval system and the main source used for this study. Essentially the same information was published in the *Table des constructions des principaux matériels d'artillerie* (Paris, 1792).

Susane, Louis, *Histoire de l'artillerie française* (Paris, 1874). Especially useful for artillery units.

Tousard, Louis de, *American Artillerist's Companion, or Elements of Artillery* (Philadelphia, 1809), 2 volumes of text and an atlas of plates. A most valuable and detailed account of the Gribeauval system and British mid-18th century artillery, both types of guns being used in the United States.

Teil, Jean du, *De l'usage de l'artillerie nouvelle dans la guerre de campagne* (Metz, 1778)

Coast guard militia artillerymen in a battery, 1772. Note the mortar at right and the guns at the left mounted on naval carriages with large wheels upon a traversing platform. (Print after Moltzheim. Anne S.K. Brown Military Collection, Brown University, USA. Photo RC)

COLOUR PLATE COMMENTARY

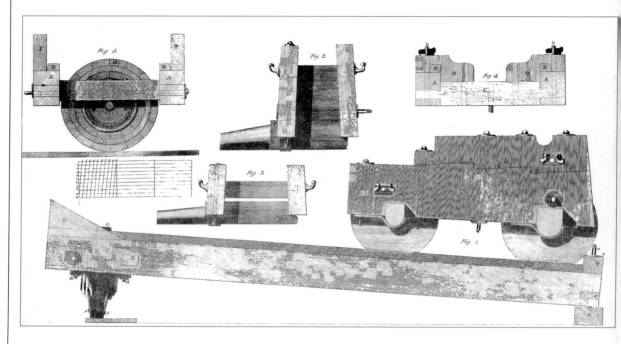

PLATE A: GRIBEAUVAL BRASS 24-PDR SIEGE GUN AND CARRIAGE

The 'battering' siege guns of Napoleon's army were the 24-pdr and the 16-pdr. For both models, Gribeauval kept basically the same proportions as the Vallière guns but without the intricate decorative mouldings. The plates illustrating Gribeauval's system show that rather than having squared handles as for the field guns, the heavy guns had dolphins (as shown). The carriages of the heavy guns were basically of the same design as those for the field artillery but were larger and reinforced to stand the strain of the gun's heavy weight. The quoin was used for aiming as the elevating screw, so useful for field artillery, was awkward with heavy guns.

1) side view.
2) top view.

PLATE B: GRIBEAUVAL LIMBER FOR HEAVY SIEGE GUNS

The 16- and 24-pdr heavy siege guns and the 8-inch siege howitzer all had the same type of limber to hook onto their carriages. The limber's total length was 8ft 7in. (278cm) and the height of the wheels was 2ft 10in. (92cm). The heavy siege artillery was often transported by wagons or boats but when it approached the town to be besieged, the guns and carriages were unloaded, assembled and hooked on to their limbers for the final part of the journey.

1) pattern of a shaft.
2) pattern of a bolster.
3) side view of limber.

Coastal artillery profile, top and rear of the carriage, and profile of the rails (or frame) it sits on with a view of the rear wheel. This arrangement was introduced in 1765 as part of the Gribeauval system. (Print after de Scheel)

4) top view of limber.
5) profile of bolster from rear.

PLATE C: GRIBEAUVAL COASTAL ARTILLERY TRAVERSING PLATFORM

The most complicated and accomplished invention concerning a gun's carriage was the system devised by Sieur Berthelot for coastal artillery batteries. It was a refinement of Gribeauval's garrison carriage for, not only did it provide rails upon which the gun's carriage could easily recoil and be pointed again, but it could 'traverse' – swing from one side to another – to follow its target. This was done by having a rail laid on the ground, the rail having the form of a semi-circle. The rear of the traversing platform had a small wheel slotted into the rail to run on the semi-circle thus allowing the carriage to traverse up to about 45 degrees at each side. With this arrangement, even the heaviest iron naval gun was moved, aimed and fired with relative ease by a few men. The early design called for a naval-type carriage with medium sized wheels (or trucks) shown here.

1) side view with 18-pdr naval gun.
2) rear wheel.
3) front of carriage.
4) rear of carriage.

PLATE D: COASTAL ARTILLERY NAVAL IRON 36-PDR GUN ON A GRIBEAUVAL TRAVERSING PLATFORM

As shown on Plate C, the early design for the coastal artillery traversing platform called for medium sized wheels. This was further refined in the late 1770s by simply putting the ship's carriage without wheels on the tracks. A long handspike – it had a flattened top and also acted as plank for a gunner to stand on – was added to the transom joining the rear of the rails to make traversing the gun easier.

The ammunition for coastal batteries consisted mainly of round solid shot (a) with a proportion of one solid shot in seven to be bar shot. This rather high amount of bar shot was because it was hoped that rigging of the enemy ship would be damaged. The three basic types of bar shot − b) the cross bar shot, c) the jointed cross bar shot, and d) the expanding bar shot – are shown.

The gunners' implements to serve the heavy guns were generally the same as those of the field artillery but were longer. There was a combination sponge and rammer implement for the siege 8- and 12-pdr guns. However, for 16- and 24-pdrs (and 36-pdrs for coast artillery) the implements were quite long and had only one function as a combination tool would make them too heavy and somewhat fragile

A naval iron gun mounted on a Gribeauval coastal artillery traversing carriage with an officer and a gunner of the coast guard artillery, 1786. This traversing platform is built with a rear wheel at the centre of the transom. From 1778, the coast guard artillery had a blue uniform with 'sea green' lapels, piping, waistcoat and breeches, along with yellow metal buttons. (Print after Marbot. Anne S.K. Brown Military Collection, Brown University, USA. Photo RC)

PLATE E: GRIBEAUVAL GARRISON CARRIAGE FOR A BRASS 16-PDR

This type of carriage was based upon oak rails. As can be seen, the wooden track arrangement was simply laid over the old firing platform. This both ensured that the gun could be reloaded and fired quickly, and reduced the number of artillerymen required to crew the piece. The number now needed was two gunners and three servants (or assistant gunners).

1) side view.
2) top of carriage.
3) front of carriage.
4) rear of carriage.
5) quoin.

PLATE F: MORTARS AND MORTAR BOMBS

1) 10-inch brass mortar from the 1760s. This mortar had the cylindrical chamber common to the mortars of Gribeauval's system.

2) 12-inch brass Gomer mortar from the 1780s. Note the conical chamber that was the hallmark of Gomer's design. This provided a very snug fit for the bomb so that it would not damage the sides of the chamber when fired. The trunnions each had a triangular reinforce.

3) 12-inch brass Gomer mortar for coastal artillery from the early 1800s. This mortar has the same conical chamber, but the trunnions have moved to the breech.

4) 12-inch coastal artillery mortar cast with its base plate, cast in 1799 at Toulon. The base plate was bolted to blocks of wood held with iron straps.

Mortar bombs were hollowed projectiles weighing some 50kg to 75kg designed to explode above their target. The bomb's lower part was reinforced but there was always the danger that it would explode as it was shot. The mortar would be damaged or destroyed, its servants killed or wounded. Each bomb had a fuse. This was made from the hollowed pipe of a lime tree and filled with an inflammable

A naval iron 24-pdr on a Gribeauval coastal artillery carriage and traversing platform. The platform had two wheels, one at each rear corner, which was more common with the heavier calibre guns. The naval carriage has no wheels and the recoil slid it backwards on its axles. The coast guard artillery corps blue and sea green uniforms of the officer and gunner are of 1786. (Print after Moltzheim. Anne S.K. Brown Military Collection, Brown University, USA. Photo RC)

mixture. The timing of how long it would take to burn in order to explode was estimated by a senior bombardier or artificer. Gribeauval conceived bombs with two rings to allow easier transport of these heavy projectiles.

5) 12-inch bomb, top view. 6) 12-inch bomb profile. 7) 10-inch bomb, side view. 8) 10-inch bomb, section profile.

PLATE G: 10-INCH GRIBEAUVAL MORTAR WITH ITS BED

1) side view of mortar mounted on its bed. 2) resting board. 3) cutaway of a 10-inch mortar.

A 24-pdr naval gun on a coastal traversing carriage, 1790s. (Print after Martinet)

BELOW **Senior gunner, coast guard artillery, 1810–13. Print by Vernet and Lami, contemporary artists, showing the blue uniform with sea green facings and red epaulettes. The shako has a red pompon. The cartridge box badge is the corps insignia: an anchor with crossed guns.**

Firing a mortar was a very complicated and dangerous occupation. The 10-inch mortar shown here was possibly the handiest such piece of ordnance in Napoleon's armies. Of a new calibre introduced by Gribeauval, it was light enough, as mortars go, to be brought along as siege artillery as well as being useful for defending a fortress. The mortar shown here is Gribeauval's basic design with a cylindrical chamber.

First, the powder had to be loaded. Five men were required to serve a 10-inch or a 12-inch mortar. The mortar tube was placed in a vertical position, as if shooting directly up. A gunner poured the powder in the chamber. This could be in a prepared charge contained in a cartridge or a calculated amount of powder poured out of a bucket. To load the bomb, the mortar's crew, from one to four men to carry the bomb depending on its weight, put the projectile in the chamber, centring it with the wooden stocks that were driven in. Once the bomb was in place, the mortar was slanted to approximately 45 degrees. It was then aimed by a bombardier and this operation demanded great skill. If done with the required skill, and a dose of good luck, a successful firing would result.

LEFT **Detail of the vent on the 12-inch iron naval mortar. (Fort Ticonderoga. Photo RC)**

INDEX